A Name for Himself

JOYCE BARKHOUSE

A Name for Himself

A BIOGRAPHY OF
THOMAS HEAD RADDALL

• NATURAL HERITAGE BOOKS •

TORONTO

Copyright © Natural Heritage/Natural History Inc.

All rights reserved. No part of this publication may be reproduced, stored in a retrieval system or transmitted in any form or by any means, electronic, mechanical, photo-copying, recording or otherwise, without the prior written permission of the publisher, Natural Heritage, P.O. Box 69, Station H, Toronto, Ontario M4C 5H7

Previously published, 1986, by Irwin Publishing Inc.

Canadian Cataloguing In Publication Data
Barkhouse, Joyce, 1913 -
   A name for himself

Rev. ed.
ISBN 0 -920474 -58 -6

1. Raddall, Thomas H., 1903-   - Biography.
2. Novelists, Canadian (English)   - 20th century - Biography.*   I. Title.

PS8535.A33Z58   1990   C813'.54   C90 - 093639-8
PR9199.3.R33Z58   1990

Every effort has been made to locate and acknowledge the correct copyright owners. Quotations from *In My Time, His Majesty's Yankees*, and *Hangman's Beach* by Thomas Head Raddall have been used with the permission of the author and The Canadian Publishers, McClelland and Stewart, Toronto.

The author gratefully acknowledges the support of the Ontario Arts Council.

Cover Design: Steve Eby

Cover photo: Thomas Raddall, in his study at the height of his career. Courtesy, Dalhousie University Archives.

Printed and bound in Canada by Imprimerie Gagné Ltée

In memory of Fred

C O N T E N T S

The Great Expolosion   *1*
Childhood   *8*
The Young Telegrapher   *22*
Rough Passages   *31*
Sable Island   *36*
Manhood   *43*
To Be a Writer   *51*
Decision   *62*
The Price of Success   *70*
A Name for Himself   *77*
Appendix   *83*
  Honours and Awards   *83*
  Novels   *84*
  Short Story Collections   *85*
  Juvenile   *85*
  Histories   *85*
  Memoir   *85*

FOREWORD

"If I live through this war I hope to see you graduate at Varsity. In any case take the ideal for the goal, and strive to make a name for yourself."

These were the last words his father wrote to Thomas Raddall, Jr., just before he was killed on the battlefield of Amiens in 1918. Tom was only fourteen years old. He never did graduate from Varsity. He was forced to leave school and go to work at once, to support himself and to help his family. But he never forgot his father's words.

Today he is known as one of Canada's greatest storytellers.

Born in Hythe, England, Tom moved to Nova Scotia with his family when he was ten years old. His early life was marked by tragedy. A few months before his father was killed, he had lived through the terrible Halifax Explosion of December, 1917. Some tough experiences followed. He became a marine telegrapher at the age of fifteen, and served at sea for more than two years before he was posted to remote Sable Island — that desert in the sea, far off the coast of Nova Scotia. He was there when he had his first short story published, at the age of eighteen — a ghost story called *The Singing Frenchman*.

Disenchanted with the life of a telegrapher, Tom took a business course in Halifax, and bought himself an old typewriter. He was working as bookkeeper for a paper mill in Liverpool, Nova Scotia, when he took the unprecedented step of giving up his nine-to-five job to devote himself, full time, to writing.

At that time no Canadian author of fiction had been able to earn even a subsistence income. Tom had a wife and two small children to support. But Tom dared, and he succeeded. This is the story of his courage, his suffering, and his successes. Out of the loneliness and despair of his stay on Sable Island, eventually he wrote one of his greatest novels, *The Nymph and the Lamp*.

Three times winner of the Governor General's award for literature, Dr. Thomas Head Raddall has received almost every honour Canada can bestow on an author. His stories are read in countries all over the world. He has made a name for himself.

ACKNOWLEDGEMENTS

The author is deeply grateful to Dr. Thomas Head Raddall for his generosity and patience in helping to prepare this brief story of his life. Special thanks also to Dr. Charles Armour, University Archivist, Dalhousie University.

CHAPTER 1

The Great Explosion

To fourteen-year-old Thomas Raddall the fateful morning of the sixth of December, 1917, began like any other day. He sat down to a breakfast of hot oatmeal porridge with his mother and his little sister, Winifred. The baby, Hilda, was in her high chair and his older sister, Nellie, was upstairs in bed with a bad cold. Tom's father was somewhere in Europe on the battlefront fighting in the World War which, it was said, would end all wars.

The family could not know that in Halifax Harbour, a short distance away, two ships were rapidly approaching each other on a deadly collision course. The incoming French freighter *Mont Blanc* was a floating munitions magazine packed below decks with picric acid and TNT, the most powerful explosives then known. Because of human error she was about to be rammed by a Belgian relief ship, the *IMO*, and would explode in a blast resulting in instant death and destruction never equalled on earth — until many years later when an atomic bomb was deliberately dropped on Hiroshima.

A few minutes before nine o'clock Thomas Raddall picked up his books and walked down the street to nearby Chebucto School. He was warmly dressed because there was a war-time shortage of fuel in the city

(Courtesy Dalhousie University Archives, Thomas Raddall Papers)
Tom was at this school on Chebucto Road when the Halifax Explosion occurred.

and the janitor was under orders to bank the fire in the coal furnace every night. Only the oldest students in the top class, Grade Nine, had to attend at the usual hour. All the others came at ten o'clock, when the classrooms were warmer.

Thomas was not fond of school but he liked his teacher, the headmaster, Mr. Marshall — known as Old Gander because of his long skinny neck and bald head. He had a thick white moustache and intelligent blue eyes shaded by bushy eyebrows. Tom had just flung his books on his desk and taken his seat when Mr. Marshall rapped out,

"Attention!"

This was the command for all of the students to stand by their desks in military fashion, eyes front.

"Let us sing the morning hymn," said Mr. Marshall, and Tom joined in lustily.

"Awake my soul and with the sun
Thy daily stage of duty run, . . ."

"Be seated," said the teacher, at the end of the verse, and at that moment the *Mont Blanc* exploded.

Many years later Thomas Raddall described what happened:

> . . . we felt two distinct shocks. The first was a sort of earthquake in which the floor seemed to rise and drop. . . . A few seconds later the air blast smote us. In the same order there were two tremendous noises, first a deep grumble from the ground and then an ear-splitting bang . . . It was like being shaken by a maniac giant with one fist and then slammed on your head with the other. I was able to move and talk rationally, but the concussion left me in a dazed state for many hours, during which I regarded strange and horrible sights as calmly as if they happened every day.
>
> The effects in the classroom were swift and destructive. The windows vanished . . . Behind my row of desks a door-glass tipped forward, shot horizontally over our heads, and sliced deeply into the wall in front of us . . . The big clock on the wall just missed the headmaster and shattered on his desk. All the plaster sprang off the walls in large and small chunks, and filled the room with a fog of white dust. We jumped to our feet, staring at each other. One girl screamed (her cheek was cut from mouth to ear), . . . For a few seconds we stood like a lot of powdered clowns with badly applied daubs of red paint here and there; then with the instinct born of routine fire-practice the boys and girls dived through their cloakrooms, snatching coats and headgear off the hooks or off the floor and clattering away downstairs to run home.

All except one. Tom Raddall remained standing by his desk, staring at his teacher, awaiting his command. He felt no pain from various small cuts, although his left hand was bleeding badly.

Mr. Marshall peered dazedly back at him.

"Thomas — is that you, Thomas?" he queried, and the boy answered,

"Yes, sir."

Stunned and shocked, the old man tried to think what could have happened.

"Maybe — maybe some little boys were playing with dynamite in the basement," he stammered.

"Yes, sir," said Tom.

"We must search the building," said his teacher. "I shall look downstairs. You go through the classrooms on this floor. If you find anybody injured, or see any sign of fire, come to me at once."

Tom obeyed and found every room littered with wreckage but empty of human life. When he had finished his inspection, he rejoined the headmaster in the first-floor hallway. Mr. Marshall had just come up from the lower floor and basement where he found no sign of life. Together they went outside and saw a great pillar of cloud rising against the blue sky, forming a huge and ever-growing black and white mushroom that hung ominously over the stricken city.

Across the street a row of wooden houses seemed to look back at them with blind and empty eyes, for every window was shattered and gone. In the eerie silence which had followed the great explosion, Tom suddenly realized that his own home must have met with disaster. What had happened to his family?

He ran across the street to where a team of horses lay, still harnessed to the shafts of an oil wagon. The driver was kneeling between them — a hand on each head. The man looked up in bewilderment.

"Would you think a man could stand a thing that killed a horse?" he asked, but Tom had no answer. His one thought now was to get home.

"Mother! Mother!" he called, for he found his home like the school, littered with plaster and splinters of glass and wood. Rags of curtains were waving in the cold breeze where the windows should have been. There, in the garden, he found his sisters, Nellie, Winifred, and Hilda unhurt, although Nellie had had a miraculous escape from death. Her bedroom was on the north side of the house — the side from which the blast had come. Pieces of glass from the window had flown over her head with such violence that some of the shards went completely through the closed door. When she came to her senses she got out of bed and ran downstairs in her bare feet, over glass and rubble, without getting a scratch.

But Tom's mother had a bad cut, which was streaming blood, on her forehead, and a great sliver of glass protruded from her breast. She pulled it out herself and a gush of blood followed. Tom ran out into the street where he stopped the driver of a truck and begged him to take her to the hospital. Within an hour she was back home again, hastily treated and bandaged, for there was little time and no room for the walking wounded.

By this time the Raddalls knew the cause of the explosion. Somehow it was better to know that a munitions ship had blown up, than to believe that the city was being bombed by the Germans, as Mrs. Raddall had at first supposed.

With his mother hurt and his older sister ill, Tom found himself the only able-bodied person in the home. He tied a rag around the cut on his left hand and set to work to try to make the kitchen habitable. He found

(Public Archives, Nova Scotia)
Soldiers of the Home Guard, like these, accompanied Thomas to Chebucto School on the night after the great explosion.

pieces of carpet and nailed them over the windows. But that night the temperature fell, the wind arose, and a howling blizzard sent snow sifting through every crack between the nails that held the pieces in place. While the family huddled around the stove to keep from freezing, a knock came and a man's voice called out,

"Anybody here?"

Tom and his mother went into the hall. A soldier stood in the entrance where the front door had blown off. He had been told that there was a boy in the house who could take him to Chebucto School and show him around. Tom went with him and led the way down the concrete steps into the undamaged basement.

The soldier muttered,

"Hold a thousand, easy."

Tom didn't know what he meant, but as he stood around, wondering what to do next, the first horse-drawn load of bodies arrived. He watched, paralyzed with horror, as by the dim light of a kerosene lantern, soldiers dropped one dreadfully mutilated body after another in a row along the basement floor of his school. At last somebody paused in this grisly business, noticed the young boy, and told him to go home.

During that awful day and night Thomas Raddall left his childhood behind him forever. Years afterward he would wonder why he alone remained at his desk that morning when all the other children ran home. He said he thought it must have been his "military" upbringing and the stern discipline of his father.

But it was more than that. The very fibre of his being made him the hero of Chebucto School. Always he would stand firm in the face of physical danger, and for what he believed to be morally right.

CHAPTER 2

Childhood

The winter that followed the Great Explosion of 1917 was a bitter one in the stricken city of Halifax. Compared to some families, the Raddalls might have been considered lucky, because no one had been killed or seriously injured, the house had not been flattened and the kitchen stove still worked. A neighbour came and helped to board up broken windows and make other temporary repairs. All the same, it was a dreary, miserable time. Shivering with cold, Tom had to be the first to get up every morning to light the smoky coal fire. Then he trudged off through wind, snow or sleet to deliver newspapers before he went back to the uncomfortable, make-shift school. At home he had to assume every heavy duty. As his mother reminded him, he was the only man in the house.

One thought, one hope was always with him. Some day the War would be over, the Allies would win, and his father would come home.

Early childhood memories had already begun to take on dream-like qualities for Tom. These memories were of the military, sea-side town of Hythe, in England, where he had been born in November of 1903. At that time his father had been a warrant-officer and an instructor in sharp-shooting in the School of Musketry, so Tom had been born into a military way of life. At home his father, a stern, handsome man, ruled his household with the iron discipline practised in the army. He expected his son to be a man when he was still only a child. Instant, unquestioning obedience was demanded from every member of the family.

Sometimes Tom hated his father for being so unreasonably strict. But he admired and respected him as well, and at times they shared a special comradeship. Some of his earliest and happiest memories of England were of the occasions when he had been taken as the only passenger on his father's bicycle, perched proudly on a cushion attached to the handlebars. In this way father and son had visited some very famous nearby places. Captain Raddall loved history and he knew how to make it come alive in the telling. Tom's eyes grew big and his heart beat faster when they entered places like mysterious Saltwood Castle, where King Henry's courtiers had plotted to murder Thomas à Becket at Canterbury ". . . the men all sitting in the dark so none might see another's face." Small Tom's vivid imagination peopled the whole countryside around Hythe with ghosts of the past.

Tom was nine years old when the quiet and familiar way of life in England came to an abrupt end. One day his father came home to make a startling announcement.

"Pack up your most precious belongings," he told the children. "We are going to leave England and go to Canada to live."

They were dumbfounded.

"I applied for this move," said Captain Raddall, "because I believe I'll have opportunities for advancement in my military career if I take a Canadian post. And I believe that you, my children, will have opportunities for better lives in Canada."

Far from being upset, Tom was thrilled. Visions of tracking moose through unknown forests, of hunting buffaloes on vast open prairies, of sleeping in wigwams with Indians and learning from them the lore of the wilderness flashed into his mind. No more dull old lessons at Saint Leonard's School for Boys!

Tom knew all about North America — or thought he did. In the past couple of years he had been allowed to go to the "flickers" — silent black and white movies at the local theatre, every Saturday night. Tom loved the Westerns, and soon discovered he could learn even more about outlaws and Indians and cowboys from "penny dreadfuls," which he could buy at the local bookshop. These cheap paperback booklets offered a whole series on the fantastic adventures of Buffalo Bill. Tom spent every penny of his allowance trying to collect them all.

His mother became alarmed at her son's low taste in reading and complained to his father. Tom listened in fear to the conversation, because if his father said "no more Buffalo Bill" then that would be the end of his world of fantasy. But his father only smiled and said,

"Don't worry about it, Ellen. It's better for him to read harmless trash than not to read at all. He'll soon discover better things on our bookshelves and at the library."

And Tom did. By the time the family set sail for Canada he had become an avid reader, and had been on many a famous imaginary adventure. He had been shipwrecked on a desert island with Robinson Crusoe; he had prowled the jungles of India with Kim and Mowgli; and — best of all — he had slipped silently

(Courtesy Dalhousie University Archives, Thomas Raddall Papers)
Thomas and Ellen Raddall with Nellie, Tom, and Winnifred, in 1912.

through the forests of North America on beaded moccasins, well-oiled rifle at the ready, with Pathfinder and Deerslayer.

The Raddalls could take very few of their possessions with them, but Tom rejoiced as he helped to pack all the books from their library.

His heart sank, however, as he watched their big, old walnut piano with swinging brass candle-brackets on each side of the music rack, being crated and boxed. He hated the piano and he hated his father for forcing him to take lessons. Music was one of his father's great pleasures. He loved to sing and put on amateur entertainments. Tom was musical, too, but his fingers weren't long enough and his square hands weren't the right shape to make a really good pianist. He was glad to leave behind forever his piano teacher, "a cruel old ape-faced man with side-whiskers," who beat time with a silver-tipped baton which he also used to whack Tom's fingers every time he made a mistake.

Tom made a lot of mistakes. His sister, Nellie, had lovely long-tapered fingers. She seldom made mistakes, so her fingers weren't whacked. It wasn't fair.

"But maybe," thought Tom, as he saw the piano go out of the door of his home in Hythe, "maybe there won't be any piano teachers in Halifax, Nova Scotia. In Canada, the land of cowboys and Indians, there will be an entirely new way of life."

But Halifax proved to be a bitter disappointment. It was a mean, grubby-looking town, with a huddle of shabby wooden buildings clustered together on a steep slope overlooking the Harbour. A few of the streets were cobbled, but most were dirt. Horses' hooves raised clouds of dust in fine weather and spattered pedestrians with mud when it rained

And the new way of life was certainly not as pleasant as the one he had so happily abandoned in England. The Raddalls moved into a small rented house on Chebucto Road near the school. The new home had running water and a bathroom but no electric light. Tom read and studied by the light of a kerosene lamp or a candle.

It was hard to make new friends in this dreary place. Worst of all, his father wasted no time in finding a piano teacher. This time it was Miss Hoyt, an elderly spinster who gave lessons in her own home. Twice a week Tom had to walk from the north to the south end of the city, carrying a music case. This marked him out not only as a new kid, but also as a sissy. He became the sport of a gang of tough boys along the route who soon learned what time he had to go for his lessons and lay in wait for him in different places along the way.

Tom was no sissy. He had a quick temper and hard fists when he was seething with anger and resentment. It was useless for him to complain to his inflexible father, so some of the bullies learned to respect his ability to fight his own battles against heavy odds.

Tom hated the whole music thing. In addition to the lessons at Miss Hoyt's, he had to spend an hour practising at home every afternoon or evening when his friends were out having fun. And it was all so useless. All the lessons and all the practicing could not alter the shape or size of his hands and fingers, which were much better suited to those of a sailor . . . The worst of his musical ordeals, however, were Miss Hoyt's annual "recitals." Nellie loved to get dressed up in frilly gowns and glide up to the platform where she performed flawlessly and all the ladies smiled approval and ap-

14

(Courtesy Dalhousie University Archives, Thomas Raddall Papers)
Tom, at the age of ten, proudly wearing his military cadet uniform.

plauded enthusiastically. Tom loathed being dressed up and made to perform, as if he was a poor miserable monkey that an organ grinder put through degrading routines on street corners. He felt like one of those monkeys when he had to stumble shame-facedly, onto the platform and make a mess of his solo. At the end of his performance, he had to make a stiff bow and walk back to his seat to the humiliating sound of a few feeble handclaps from the audience. Tom vowed to himself that when he was grown up and could do as he pleased, he would never dress up and perform for anybody.

As soon as the family was established in Halifax, Captain Raddall took up his duties, giving lectures and demonstrations at Wellington Barracks and at the Armouries. That fall, young Tom also became a part of the military establishment when he joined the cadet corps of the Halifax school. He liked this. He felt proud and important when he wore a uniform with brass buttons and a broad-brimmed mountie hat and learned to shoot with a .22 calibre rifle. He excelled at this, and he hoped to become an expert sharpshooter, like his father.

In the summer of 1914, Captain Raddall took Tom with him to a militia camp on fortified McNab's Island at the entrance to Halifax Harbour. This was a happy experience for Tom, which he never forgot. Much of the time he was allowed to explore the length and width of the five-kilometre long island. At last he could tramp through the woods and play at cowboys and Indians.

But Tom wasn't satisfied just to look around and play games. Whenever the boy met local inhabitants — fishermen and their families lived on the island — he would pester them with questions about the place. That way he learned how the first Peter McNab — for whom the island was named — had built a handsome stone mansion at the top of the hill, where now big guns pointed seaward to protect the city of Halifax from possible invaders. Most memorable was a long stony beach which was pointed out to him as the place where admirals of the Royal Navy had once ordered the gibbeting of the tarred bodies of sailors who had been hanged or flogged to death for mutiny or desertion.

"Why were the bodies tarred?" Tom wanted to know.

"To make 'em last longer, so as the birds wouldn't peck at 'em. They was hanged there in plain view of every warship comin' or goin', as a warning to all the sailors as to what would happen to them if they didn't obey orders."

Tom shuddered. That night he lay awake, listening to the "sea muttering on the stones and a foghorn groaning where dead men used to keep watch on the harbour channel."

Tom never forgot those days of camping on McNab's Island and he never forgot the haunting tales, he had heard, of people who had lived there more than a century and a half before. Long afterwards, when he was past middle age and already a famous writer, he would explore the island again, before he sat down to write a novel that he called *Hangman's Beach*. He could vividly imagine scenes of the past. They were as real to him as if he had actually been there.

. . . A fine sunset made a huge red splash over the western sky, and cast on the harbour channel the growing black shadow of York Redoubt. . . .

Some time and distance before McNab set foot on the sea-polished stones at the tip of the point, he saw the object of his curiosity well enough, but he went on and stepped ashore to note the details. A tall post of eight-by-eight timber had been set up, with a massive cairn of beach stones piled about the foot to hold it

17

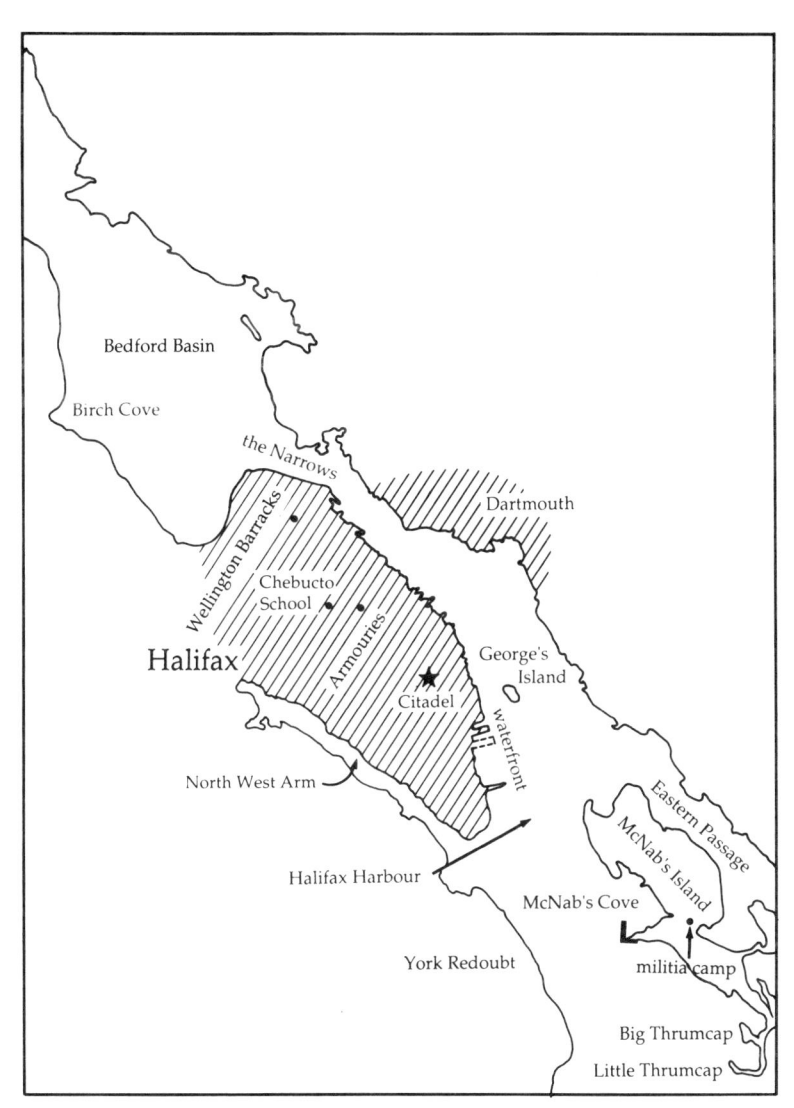

(Public Archives, Nova Scotia. Adapted.)
Halifax and McNab's Island
Tom spent an exciting summer exploring McNab's Island. Later, as a young man, he passed much time at the Halifax waterfront. There he learned about the kind of people and the way of life he used in many of his stories. This map also shows the Narrows where the two ships collided to cause the great explosion of 1917.

against any wind that blew. At the top of the post, a height of two fathoms, a short arm of the same timber jutted at a right-angle, and from it hung the naked body of a man, daubed with tar from head to foot. A few links of chain and an iron collar about his neck held him to the beam. His wrists were shackled together, and so were his ankles. The wood was new, with fresh chips lying about, and tar spattered on the stones. The feathery ashes of a driftwood fire showed where the tar pot had been heated.

Even as a ten year old, in spite of it not being the wide open country of his dreams, Tom felt a growing sense of excitement as he realized the raw, new country of Canada already had a history of her own. That summer when he returned to Halifax after his happy vacation he looked at the shabby city with new vision. Maybe Halifax had a romantic history, too.

But, as it happened, there was no time then for thinking about the past. It was 1914. Bad news had come from England. Dark clouds of war had been gathering over Europe and now it was certain the storms would break. Tom's father was sent to a training camp in Calgary. He was there in August when Germany attacked France. The First World War had begun.

Captain Raddall might have remained safely in Canada as an instructor, but such was not his way. He applied at once for active service and was appointed machine-gun officer for the Winnipeg Rifles. He sailed from Quebec in September without having a chance to say good-bye to his family. In April of the following year he was wounded in the head and arm at Ypres, and by June he was back in Halifax, on convalescent leave.

When Tom first learned that his father had gone to the battlefront, he felt a guilty sense of relief because he would no longer have to endure his father's harsh discipline. But when he found out that his father had been seriously wounded, he was filled with a wrenching emotion he couldn't understand. Was it possible to love and hate somebody at the same time? When Captain Raddall came home in 1915, Tom saw him as a different man:

> After his experience in the shambles of Flanders there was a change in him. He was a man of middle height, lean and muscular, with keen grey eyes in a face that seemed cast in a stern bronze mould. Now this mask dissolved and revealed to me a new and warm personality. He drew me into talks about my interests and studies and took me on walks about Halifax, pointing out places of historical interest, all in a spirit of comradeship that delighted me.
> . . . Father talked to me about my future. He also sought out and talked to my teachers. I was no student at all in the academic sense. I cared for nothing much but history and English composition . . . and the only prizes I won at school were for essays. . . .

Once while his father was home on leave, Tom overheard him say to his mother,

"I think the boy should go in for journalism. He seems to have a definite bent."

Tom felt a thrill of gladness. He had been afraid that his father would force him to go in for a musical career.

At the end of his convalescence, Captain Raddall was asked to stay in Canada and continue the work he had begun as a recruitment officer, but he felt it his duty to again enter active service at the Front. So Tom said a troubled good-bye to the father who had become his companion and friend.

> He left us to return to the War on a sunny day in August of 1915 . . . He engaged a smart pony-trap to take him to the railway station. He was smiling as he kissed us all good-bye but his eyes were full of tears, like ours

. . . I have always felt that some . . . instinct told him that this was the last time he would see his family. I can still see the trap trotting away, the driver flicking his whip and the man in khaki dabbing at his eyes with a handkerchief . . . Three years later, almost to the day, he was lying dead on the battlefield of Amiens.

Tom was at home when the tragic news came. It was only eight months after the Halifax Explosion at a time when everyone knew that the War was almost over, with victory on the side of the Allies. Many times Tom had imagined the joyous moment when he would see his father again. It would never happen.

His sisters wept with their mother, but Tom had no tears. He went out alone and sat on the doorstep in the sunlight. Although he had been brought up in a devout Christian home, he could not pray. He could not believe that an all-powerful and all-merciful God would permit the awful suffering he had witnessed after the Explosion, or the agony and death of a good man like his father on the battlefield. Filled with bitterness, anger, and grief, he vowed he would never trust either God or man, but would be totally responsible for himself.

Many years later he wrote a poem for his lost father:

Where the dead lay thickest, there they found
My father with the sunset on his face
Amid the wheat. There was a cheerful sound
Of skylarks, nothing else, as if that place
Had never known a battle. The dead lay
As athletes fling themselves to earth at last.
The trampled wheat, the shattered roofs of Caix.
And these, marked where the regiment had passed.
He was their Colonel, they had loved him well. . . .

Tom had loved him well, too. He grieved for him for

the rest of his life, and always kept his last letter, in which his father had written at the end:

> If I live through this war I hope to see you graduate at Varsity. In any case take the ideal for your goal and strive to make a name for yourself.

CHAPTER 3

The Young Telegrapher

Soon after her husband's death, Mrs. Raddall had a heart-to-heart talk with Tom and Nellie. She told them that their father's dream of University for them both could never come true. She had learned that her pension as a war widow would amount to only $85.00 a month, with an additional small allowance for each child under the age of fifteen. Nellie was seventeen and Tom would be fifteen in November.

Actually, Major T.H. Raddall, DSO, had been promoted to the rank of Lieutenant-Colonel overseas, but through neglect this rank had not been recorded at the time. Later, when the error was corrected, his widow would receive an additional few dollars.

But, as Tom said:

> Mother found herself in a frightening position in that last autumn of the War. Rent, food, clothing, fuel, everything necessary for existence had rocketed since the War began, and now the cost was climbing faster than ever. . . Father's cash savings had been pitifully small. . . Her one hope was to return to England, where her Canadian pension dollars would buy more, but while the War lasted (this) was impossible. . . .

Faced with the prospect of leaving school at once to find work, Nellie was devastated. She had always excelled at school. She and her best friend, Helene Sandford, had planned and dreamed that they would enter Dalhousie University together. Now Nellie had to agree that she would take a short course in shorthand and typing and become a stenographer.

As for Tom, he had always hated school. In spite of his sister's tears and his mother's despair, he couldn't hide his joy.

He had never been a real wage-earner. The summer before he had laboured on a farm as a *Soldier of the Soil* to "Help Win the War" but he had received no pay and very poor board. As for his paper route, he had been trying for over a year to save enough money to buy a second-hand bicycle.

Now he was about to become independent. For the moment he almost forgot his grief over his father's death.

His mother had one suggestion. She said that when Tom's father had been home on leave in 1915 he had talked to William Dennis, owner of the *Halifax Herald*. He told Mr. Dennis that Tom had a flair for writing and that if "anything happened" he hoped Tom would get an opportunity to go in for journalism. Mr. Dennis had immediately promised that "if anything happened" he would see that the boy got a chance with the *Herald*.

Tom was elated. He certainly didn't mind quitting school in Grade Ten, and he was thrilled that his father had made arrangements for him to start work in the field he liked best. Thomas Head Raddall, Junior, was going to be a journalist!

He set off for the *Herald* offices on Sackville Street with a high heart. There, he gave his message to one of the girls who took it into the office of Mr. Dennis. She came back with word that Mr. Dennis was too busy to see him that day. So Tom went home and came back the next day — and the next — always with the same result.

What was to become of him? He had set his whole heart on becoming a journalist. He tried the only other Halifax paper, the *Morning Chronicle*, where the editorial manager offered him a job — out of pity — as an office boy. Sweeping floors and running errands was not what the proud Tom had in mind. He said "Thank you" and left.

He hated to go home again and tell his mother about his bad luck. As he stood in the street, hesitating, he looked up and saw a sign which read:

CANADIAN SCHOOL OF TELEGRAPHY

He stared at it disconsolately, and then suddenly he remembered that when he had been studying the newspaper ads under "Jobs Available" he had read one which said, "Telegraphers Wanted." It stated that there was a special demand for wireless-telegraph operators in the Merchant Marine. Tom's first encounter with a wireless operator had been aboard the steamer, *Carthaginian*, in which the family had sailed from Liverpool. Attracted by mysterious crackling noises, he had peered into the small steel cabin bolted to the upper deck and seen a person, wearing steel head phones, pounding a heavy brass object that made sparks.

The very thing! What he really wanted — he decided in that moment — was to get away from his sad home, to travel to far exotic places, meet interesting people, see the world. He went inside. The fee for the wireless course at the School of Telegraphy was eighty dollars.

Tom ran home and begged his mother to let him take the course. She was appalled. Eighty dollars! It might as well have been eighty thousand. It would take nearly all her savings. She read the brochure he had brought home, and noted at once that the minimum age for a first-class, sea-going certificate was eighteen. Tom was not yet fifteen. It was out of the question.

But Tom was wildly enthusiastic. He would not give in.

"I can lie about my age. Lots of boys and girls got into the army when they were only fifteen or sixteen. Father said so."

"But, Tom, what if you are caught? The money will be gone and you may end up with nothing."

"I won't get caught, Mother. And I'll work hard, I promise you. I know I'll like telegraphy. I'll do my very best, and I'll pay you back as soon as I get work—every cent."

Looking at her son's shining eyes and eager face, Mrs. Raddall could no longer refuse. She gave him the fee and he began his studies at the School of Telegraphy.

Tom memorized the international alphabet in the dot-and-dash code in no time. Then he practised day after day, week after week, often going back at night to work at the heavy brass radio-telegraph key. He had to work up to a speed of twenty words a minute in order to get a First Class Certificate. He also had to learn how to install and repair all kinds of equipment, and memorize all the wireless traffic rules for an operator-at-sea.

Before he had finished the course, the Armistice that officially ended the War was signed, but Canadian shipyards were continuing to build steam freighters mostly for the new Canadian Government Merchant Marine. This fleet was known as the "Rat Line," because the Canadian ships flew the British merchant jack with the addition of a beaver. (Sailors the world over would shout with laughter when they saw a rodent on the Canadian flag.)

(Courtesy CN Historical Services)
The house flag of the Canadian Government Merchant Marine Ltd. c. 1920. The flag was 12ft. x 6ft. The design consisted of a Greek Cross in blue on a white ground. A yellow anchor was shown on the centre ball, and the Canadian beaver was displayed in the upper staff quarter.

Because of a new law, all the "Rat" ships needed wireless operators, familiarly known as Sparks or Brasspounders, and Tom couldn't wait to get aboard. Early in the spring of 1919 he took his examinations. Written papers, including his birth certificate and the report of the examining officers at Halifax, had to be sent to Ottawa. When it came time to fill out the accompanying form, he hesitated before he filled in date of birth. His mother, watching him, said awkwardly,

"Wait, Tom. You mustn't put November 14. Actually you were born on November 13, but I—we—well, it's such an unlucky number I decided you should always celebrate on the 14th."

Tom looked up at his mother's flushed face in astonishment. Then he burst out laughing.

"Well, I'm not superstitious, Mother. I'll make my own good luck. You'll see!"

Tom really hoped the examiners at Ottawa wouldn't notice that he was actually two and a half years younger than the "18" he had written as his age on his exam paper. They, however, were not so careless as that. The discrepancy was noted, but his marks were so high he was issued a Second Class Certificate. Second Class meant he could serve as Junior Operator in ships carrying more than one operator, or he could take sole charge on trawlers, colliers, and small tramp steamers.

Since there was a shortage of trained men, he was hired by the Marconi Company at once. He had a short stint ashore before he signed aboard the *War Karma*, on May 17, 1919, as Junior Wireless Operator. The Canadian built *War Karma* was an iron steamer which belonged to the British Ministry of Transport. Tom really wanted to serve with the Canadian Government Merchant Marine, under the "Rat" flag, but he was happy to have a job aboard ship, and to set off on his first great adventure. It was a proud moment when he donned his officer's uniform resplendent with a double row of brass buttons down the front and gold braid on the cuffs. However, it didn't take him long to discover that wireless operators had little prestige. He wrote later ". . . a brasspounder was considered, and frequently told, that he was the lowest form of marine life. He sailed the seas in a chair, fiddling with knobs and switches, and making noisy electrical sparks." He was also the lowest paid. As Junior Operator Tom earned $45.00 a month.

All the same at fifteen he had a man's job, and he was determined to succeed. He was interested in the ship's name, and learned that *Karma* came from the Sanskrit, and meant "fate by deeds." This was exactly his own philosophy. He decided he would take "Karma," the name of his first ship, as his motto for life.

The senior wireless operator, a tall, gangling fellow of twenty-six — known as "Skin" because he was so thin — shared a little cabin with him across an alleyway from the radio room. At sea they had to keep continuous watch, each doing six hours on duty and six off, around the clock.

Tom described his first experience:

> The ship ran into stormy weather soon after leaving Halifax. Deeply laden, and carrying a large deck load of timber, she rolled and pitched unmercifully. For forty-eight hours or more I was miserably seasick and homesick, but I never missed a watch. Whenever Skin came to rouse me I got up at once, clenching my teeth and staggering to the radio room. For the next six hours I sat at the instruments, bracing myself against the violent movements of the ship and dutifully making a log entry every fifteen minutes, recording names of call letters of ships engaged in wireless traffic.

Although he soon overcame his seasickness and never really suffered from it again, homesickness was a different matter. He missed his mother and sisters and the quiet security of his life in Halifax more than he ever could have guessed. He began to keep a diary so he would be able to tell his family about his experiences when he got back to Halifax. In it, he included descriptions of people, details of his surroundings, his emotions and reactions — everything that was uppermost in his mind at the moment.

This was the beginning of a lifelong practice, one that would prove of inestimable value to him as an author. He had a prodigious memory, but in later life he always relied on his diary to refresh details and check facts.

A lot of wreckage from the War had been left in the North Atlantic. The wireless operators had to locate and list such things as wooden derelicts, mines that had gone adrift from their moorings, and the exact position of icebergs. They wrote their entries on long yellow sheets, which had to be mailed promptly at the end of a voyage to Canadian Marconi headquarters (ARCON) in Montreal.

ARCON controlled the fate of all Canadian wireless operators. A message from ARCON was a word from God. ARCON could snatch a man from a ship and station him ashore on some desolate island or cape in the sub-Arctic, or, if pleased with his work, might put him aboard a smart new freighter bound for far-off romantic places — Africa, India, Australia.

Tom worked conscientiously, never missing a watch.

One night the *War Karma* was caught in a violent storm, and Tom almost lost his life — but he told of the experience with humour:

> . . . I was on my way back to the radio cabin with a sandwich and a mug of hot cocoa when the ship rolled deeply to starboard, and a huge sea came out of the darkness . . . In a moment I was neck-deep in the North Atlantic and would have been dragged over the rail if I hadn't been able to fling one arm about a stanchion and hang on. After what seemed a very long time the ship recovered and rolled the other way, and I made my way, chilled and soaked, to the cabin. The sandwich was gone and so was the cocoa, but I was still clutching a mug full of sea water.

On a lovely evening in June the *War Karma* sailed up an English canal and moored at Manchester. There she lay for two weeks while the cargo was unloaded and the ship was repaired.

The crew went ashore. With the aerials lowered and coiled out of the way, there was nothing for a wireless operator to do, so Tom had the time of his life. His chosen chum was a shipmate, Walt Hunter. Before long Walt met a waitress in a café. Her girl friend also worked there, so a friendly foursome developed. Of course Tom had to pay his share of the meals and the movies for the group. Before he knew it, he had spent most of the fifty dollars his mother had given him out of her meagre income "for emergencies."

Towards the end of June the captain of the *War Karma* received orders to pay off the crew and proceed with the Canadian officers to London for reassignment. Along with most of the crew from the *Karma*, Tom and Skin were ordered to join the transport *Prince George* at Southampton. When the *Prince George* sailed for Boston, Tom was broke.

The joy of his homecoming to Halifax was dimmed when he had to confess to his mother that he could not pay her back. His guilt increased when he discovered that she had sold most of her belongings, including the piano, in his absence. She had decided that as soon as she could raise enough money she would return to England with her girls. She was sure they would be happier there.

Tom was determined to earn the money she needed. He would get a job immediately. He would not spend a cent for his own pleasure until he had repaid not only the squandered emergency fund, but also the cost of his wireless course.

CHAPTER 4

Rough Passages

To Tom's dismay he found that jobs for second-class wireless operators were no longer plentiful. He had an unpaid vacation in his partly furnished home. It was mid-August of 1919 before he was called to the Marconi office and offered a berth aboard the small freighter *Watuka*. It was a job nobody else would take. The Marconi manager told him, quite frankly, that the captain was an old tyrant who considered brasspounders to be "unnecessary, newfangled nuisances." In the one year the *Watuka* had been afloat, the captain had fired five operators.

Nevertheless Tom begged for the job. He promised he would stick it out and silently endure insults and abuses. But his heart sank the moment he met his new skipper.

> He was thickset, with a grey Edwardian beard, and he brushed wisps of thin grey hair across a balding skull. His eyes were those of a codfish, with large drooping sacs below. During the next few months I attributed these sacs to heavy drinking, . . . His upper teeth were false and cheap and ill-fitting, and their phony whiteness made a sharp contrast with the yellow snags remaining in the lower jaw.

(Courtesy Dalhousie University Archives, Thomas Raddall Papers)
Tom as wireless operator aboard the SS Watuka.

Working under this miserable man with his ill-assorted crew aboard a freighter which carried dirty cargoes such as bunker coal to East Coast Canadian ports was a far cry from Tom's dream of a happy sea-going life which would take him to "the far, the strange and the beautiful." The captain persecuted him unmercifully, giving him orders which were impossible to carry out. As the lone wireless operator Tom worked twelve hours a day, stopping only for brief meals or a quick walk on deck to stretch his cramped limbs.

One day, on a rare overseas crossing, Tom could endure it no longer. This time the captain had demanded to know what Tom had heard on the wireless from a passing liner.

"Nothing, sir," said Tom.

"Nothing!"

True to form the captain flew into a rage and began another tirade about the utter uselessness of a wireless operator, who couldn't even pick up a message from a ship in plain sight on the ocean. As he listened, Tom's anger turned into bitter resentment.

In a cold, contemptuous voice, he said,

"Passenger ships don't send messages all the time, and they have nothing to say to passing tramps."

The captain jumped to his feet and looked as if he was going to hit him. Tom stood unflinching, and listened while the man cursed him roundly, and ended with,

"Pack your baggage when we get in."

So Tom had to send a personal wireless message back to the Marconi office in Halifax, saying he had been fired.

When the ship arrived in Liverpool, England, an indignant Marconi inspector was waiting. He made a thorough check of Tom's apparatus and careful records, and then said that the captain could not discharge him on "a baseless whim."

Tom was vindicated, but not pleased. He had hoped to be sent back to Halifax on a liner and then get a post aboard another ship of the Merchant Marine. Instead he had to remain with the *Watuka*.

The captain now refused to speak to him. The unhappy Tom was still with the freighter on his sixteenth birthday. He celebrated by going ashore alone at North Sydney, Nova Scotia, to buy Christmas presents for his mother and sisters in England.

A few weeks later the captain got the punishment Tom thought he deserved. A seaman, whom he had just fired, lost his temper and in his fury might have pounded the old man to death if others had not intervened. The sailor ran below to get his belongings while the sympathetic crew passed a cap to collect money for his getaway. He had disappeared before the police arrived. The captain was taken to a hospital.

A new captain was appointed, likable Big Dan Macdonald, but within a month Tom was relieved of his arduous duties aboard the *Watuka*. After a short stint ashore at North Sydney, he was posted to a cable-repair ship. Life aboard the *Mackay-Bennett* was pleasant compared to the grim experience of the *Watuka*. Still, the business of mending cables lying at the bottom of the ocean was cold, rough, dirty work, and meant long months at sea at a stretch. The process of dragging a grapnel over the ocean floor until the cable was hooked and then hauling it to the surface could only be carried out when the ocean was reasonably calm. Tom was glad when the ship had to put into Halifax Harbour for a re-fit.

His mother and his sisters had returned to England, and he was on his own. He slept aboard ship, but he was free to prowl around and investigate the life of the waterfront. He had no taste for alcohol, but he was curious about people and the tales they had to tell, so he learned to frequent taverns and linger over a glass of whiskey and water for the sake of comradeship and a good story.

In April of 1921 Tom's work aboard the *Mackay-Bennett* came to an end, and he returned to regular Marconi service. He said:

> I had no notion of what was to come. It turned out that I had left my last ship. In the past two years I had travelled something like thirty-five thousand miles on the cold and stormy North Atlantic. No Bermuda, no Tahiti, no Hawaii . . . I bade farewell to my shipmates in the *Mackay-Bennett* with a blend of happiness and regret. I had found them good comrades afloat and ashore, mostly afloat and often in bad weather, a sure test of men in a small ship. And I had learned much about the new electronics, far beyond the needs of a mere brasspounder.
>
> Apart from that I had learned a lot about the waterfront of Halifax, where the ship had been my home. I had talked and (much more important) listened to the folk who lived there — stevedores, wharfingers, junkshop keepers, bootleggers, . . . thieves, old seamen down on their luck, boarding-house keepers — in fact all of the human medley to be found only on Water Street, of which the office and shop workers and churchgoers of the port knew nothing whatever. There was much more to learn about life, of course . . . I was still seven months short of the magic age of eighteen when I could gain my First Class Certificate and set forth to taste the world's delights as a fully qualified young man.

Meanwhile his mother had discovered that life in England was not what she had hoped for herself or for her girls. She wanted to return to Halifax and live somewhere near the old home on Chebucto Road.

CHAPTER 5

Sable Island

Tom now had a chance to repay her. During his time at sea he had saved $600.00. Now he found a house on Duncan Street listed at $5000.00 with a down payment of $500.00 and the rest to be paid in monthly instalments. His mother agreed to his making the payment, so Tom did. He arranged that the present tenants should remain until her arrival.

Now, after buying some necessary clothing and shoes, he had only a few dollars left. He was ready to go back to sea — this time, he hoped, on a voyage that would take him at last to distant and beautiful tropical islands.

But a great disappointment lay in store. When he reported to the Marconi office he was told that his next assignment was not to be at sea. He was being sent to relieve a wireless operator on Sable Island.

Sable Island!

Tom was so shocked and indignant he could hardly speak. He knew all he wanted to know about Sable Island, the "Graveyard of the Atlantic." Located two hundred seventy kilometres off the coast of Halifax, it was a desert in the sea, a sickle-shaped, treeless island, where the wind constantly shifted sand dunes to uncover parts of wrecked ships and human bones. It was

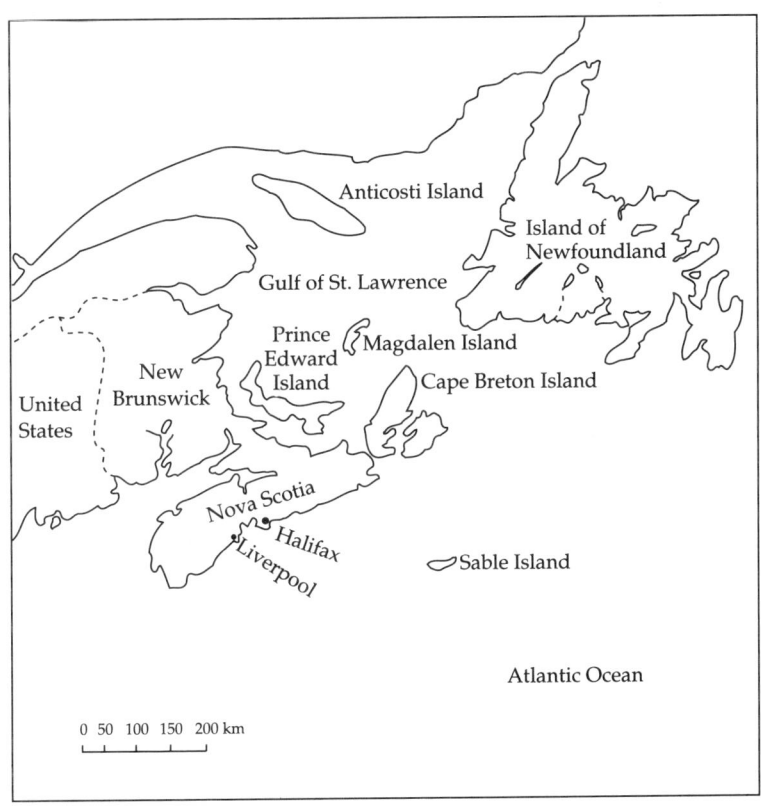

Isolated Sable Island provided the setting for one of Thomas Raddall's greatest novels, The Nymph and the Lamp.

(Nova Scotia Government Department Services)
Wild Horses on Sable Island
No one knows how the first horses arrived on Sable Island. Today they are protected by law.

inhabited by scrubby wild horses which fed on the coarse marram grass and beach pea and drank from a small freshwater inland lake. Except for sea-birds and seals, there was no other company for the wireless operators than those few families permanently settled there to operate lighthouses and lifesaving stations spaced several kilometres apart. Tom had heard stories from other operators who said they had nearly gone mad with loneliness during the year they had been forced to serve on Sable. In those days almost the only contact with the outside world — except for the dot and dash conversations on the wireless — were the quarterly annual visits of Government storeships.

Tom pleaded not to be sent to the "Graveyard," but he could not dispute the fact that he was not yet eighteen years old. He was told he had no choice but to go, or quit the Marconi service. He went, and he endured, as was his nature.

Sable Island was a noisy place. Even on calm days there was the constant booming of breakers, and when a storm sprang up the sounds were frightening. It was during such storms that the many ghosts of Sable came alive and wandered through the tumult. One was that of a French nobleman whose wife had been banished to the island by Henry IV because she had refused to become his mistress. Her husband had followed her only to discover that she was dead. He soon died of a broken heart, but it was said that often his ghost could be seen riding a big white horse through fog or foam, while on dark nights he could be heard muttering curses against the French king. This ghost caught Tom's fancy and during long, lonely hours, when the wind set up a dreadful moaning in the boiler pipes of the nearby wreck of a steamer, he wrote a story that he called *The Singing Frenchman*. He sent it to a small Halifax paper, and to his joy and astonishment it was accepted. He was a published author at the age of eighteen! Thomas Head Raddall was going to make a name for himself.

During his stay on Sable, Tom was involved in an incident for which he "made a name for himself" — at least within wireless circles — but it was not the kind of fame he was seeking. Monotony and loneliness often get the better of people stationed in isolated posts.

Nerves become edgy and quarrels are common. Tom's fight with a fellow operator — nicknamed "Sharp" — was out of the ordinary. This man was twice Tom's age and he had "the quick, mean eyes of a weasel and the disposition of a rattlesnake." He was forever bragging about how tough he was and how many men he had knocked out in fist fights.

Sharp was supposed to take over Tom's watch at midnight but he never did. Tom regularly had to go in and awaken him. The man would mutter an irritable "Okay! Okay!" but still he would not get up. Tom had to work overtime and he became more and more angry. One stormy night in January things came to a climax. Tom yanked Sharp out of his blankets onto the frosty floor, gave him a hard kick in the behind, and then went back to make the required quarter-hour log entry. Furious, Sharp ran into the watch room, grabbed Tom around the throat and started a fight which almost upset the small iron stove, full of red hot coals. Tom gasped,

"We can't fight here! We'll settle it on the beach in the morning."

He went to bed but he couldn't get to sleep. He'd been in fights before, on the waterfronts of Halifax and Sydney, but he was afraid of Sharp.

Next morning, after a silent breakfast, the man and boy went out as if for a walk along the frozen brown beach, but as soon as they were out of sight of the radio shack, they squared off. Sharp flew at Tom in a style Tom had never seen before, whirling his arms and fists like windmills while keeping his head down, with the intention of butting his opponent in the jaw. His first butt hit Tom's cheekbone, but after that it was easy to dodge the wild lunges, and Tom landed repeated hard blows of his own to the other's face. Soon Sharp's right eye was swollen shut and he was bleeding from his mouth and nose. Then Tom landed a mighty blow which struck Sharp's left eye socket just above the eye. It cut right through the eyelid which then drooped over the eye in a stream of blood. Tom was horrified. He helped the blinded man stumble back to the station, where he and the other operator applied first aid. The wound should have been stitched, for when it healed, the lid had a permanent droop.

Tom has said of the quarrel,

"After that he stood his watch on time and we got along."

The brawl became part of Sable Island legend. Word went around among the brasspounders,

"Don't fool around with young Tom Raddall. He's got a hot temper and powerful fists."

In his time off Tom spent countless hours alone, exploring the island, not always on foot. Often he borrowed a horse from one of the families who operated the three, widely spaced life-saving stations. The lifesavers had caught and trained some horses for pulling their carts or for riding patrols along the beach, but they were often unpredictable and difficult to control. More than once Tom's mount suddenly bucked or took off at a mad gallop and he was thrown to the ground. Many times he had to walk a long way back to the station.

For Tom those rides on horseback — galloping free over the rolling sand dunes, through the tall marram grass, with the wind whistling in his ears — were healing experiences. So were the walks along lonely beaches, where seals basked in the sun and sea birds circled and cried overhead. He began to feel a kinship with nature which brought relief to his young, troubled soul. For the rest of his life, he would find peace and comfort whenever he could spend time by himself — in a cabin by the sea, canoeing on a lake or tramping through the wilderness. But during the months he was forced to live in exile—often full of anger and self-pity—he never dreamed that he would look back with a certain nostalgia to that period of his life.

The day before he left, he wrote a gleeful verse:

Farewell To Sable Island

Twelve months in any place, my friends, is quite a weary while,
And seems more like a century when spent on Sable Isle.
. . . .
And when I have grown old and have grey hair beneath my cap
Before I kick the bucket with a loud and fatal rap
I'll drag my feeble limbs aboard the boat when sailing's nigh
And have another look at Sable Isle before I die.
For when I've seen the breakers pound along that sandy length
The thought of what a hell-on-earth it is will give me strength
And when the Devil lets me into Tophet with a curse,
I'll tell him, "Nick, it ain't so bad, I've seen a place that's worse!"

Today, those who read *The Nymph and the Lamp* will feel they have actually been on "Marina," so vividly does the author capture the wild, lonely, ever-changing moods of the desert in the sea.

CHAPTER 6

Manhood

When Tom had joyfully shaken the last grains of sand of Sable Island from his shoes and arrived back in Halifax, he looked forward to two things which had been promised to him before he left. First, he would have a two week vacation with his family, now happily established in the home he had found for them on Duncan Street. Second, he would be given an assignment as chief operator on board a ship of the Merchant Marine. At last he had celebrated his eighteenth birthday and was now a first-class wireless operator — in more ways than one. He could easily tap out messages with absolute accuracy at thirty words a minute!

Tom was furiously indignant when he was given only two days off duty and then ordered to go at once to Camperdown, the Marconi Station at the mouth of Halifax Harbour. It was a comparatively pleasant and easy posting, but he now had growing misgivings about his chosen career as a telegrapher. By studying and working so hard to become a top-rated operator, he had actually closed the door on life at sea. One of his friends put it in plain words.

"Anybody can pound brass aboard a ship, but expert shore station operators are scarce. As you know, nearly all the Marconi Stations along the Canadian Atlantic coast are on remote capes and islands. That's where you'll live out your days."

But Tom wouldn't.

Right then he vowed he would never spend another year of his life in isolation like that on Sable Island. He was young, and he had hardly ever had a chance to enjoy the company of his peers. He could not know that the day would come when he would long to shut himself off from the world, to be free of the nagging duties of family life, so that he could escape into the world of his imagination and live only with the people of his own creation.

And yet the seed of his ambition to become a great writer had already been planted in his unconscious mind. While at Camperdown he had bought an old second-hand typewriter for ten dollars. He really hadn't forgotten that his father had said he should have a career in journalism.

Now, for the first time since his father's death, Tom felt some relief from his financial responsibilities towards his family. His two sisters, Nellie and Winifred, had taken courses in typing and stenography. Both had found employment in Halifax. With the girls staying at home and paying board, his mother was able to keep up her monthly payments on the house without his help. All the same, she must have felt some concern when her son announced he was going to give up his secure job as a telegrapher. But Tom believed in *Karma* — fate by deeds.

He resigned from the Marconi service in mid-June. After a long bicycle trip through the pretty apple orchards and meadows of the Annapolis Valley, he stayed with his mother and sisters on Duncan Street and took a course in typing and bookkeeping at the Maritime Business College. In less than six months he had his certificate. Then he found, to his dismay, that it was a time of more depression and no jobs were available.

When he heard there was an opening for a reporter with the Canadian Press, he was filled with hope, but his application was turned down. He was stung by the reason given — lack of education. He knew that a University degree would not necessarily ensure that any person would make a good reporter. Tom hadn't even graduated from High School, but he knew he had all the essential qualifications — keen observation, a photographic memory, great curiosity about human beings and the world around him, along with the natural ability of the born storyteller to dramatize and put into words all that he observed and understood.

Tom was proud, and with his sensitive nature and retentive memory it was not easy for him ever to forget — or forgive — an injury. That polite rejection would rankle in his soul, for there was no way he could go to University and get a degree. He had to find work.

After many discouraging weeks of job hunting, he finally accepted a position at a run-down wood-pulp mill on the Mersey River in the forest of western Nova Scotia. It was another isolated place. The outlook was depressing. He promised himself he would endure it for one year — the same length of time he had served on Sable Island — and not one day more.

In fact he was to stay near the Mersey for the rest of his life.

It was not for love of his work as a clerk at the MacLeod Company at Milton, a village at the edge of the forest, about one hundred sixty kilometres west of

(Courtesy Dalhousie University Archives, Thomas Raddall Papers)
Fishing became a favourite way for Thomas Raddall to unwind.

Halifax, that he remained. Initially it was because he fell in love with the Nova Scotia wilderness.

For all his childhood delight in tales of the wild West, Tom had never been in the deep forest before. And for all his desire to emulate his father as a crack sharpshooter, he had never shot anything other than wild ducks on Sable Island. But now, because there wasn't very much to do for relaxation and amusement in Milton, he bought himself an old .22 rifle and a cheap metal fishing-rod. They proved to be his keys to paradise.

> I simply took to the woods as I had first taken to the sea. I learned to paddle a canoe and how to throw it up on my shoulders and carry it over portages. I learned to walk all day on snowshoes. I learned how to light a fire in the rain and how to use an axe, and the little Micmac crooked knife and all the other things you must know if you want to live in the woods and catch game and make yourself comfortable while you're at it.
> In these explorations and wanderings I discovered ancient Indian camp sites, and made a collection of stone arrowheads and tools, and fragments of pottery and so on. All of which set me thinking about those Fenimore Cooper books I had read when I was young. And I couldn't help laughing. He was so ridiculously wrong about so many things. As others had found before me, when Cooper wrote about ships and seamen he knew what he was talking about; but when he turned to tales of the forest he was talking through his literary hat. This taught me something that became a cardinal rule when I began to write fiction myself. Write about what you know, and know thoroughly; and never try to bluff your way through something you don't.

That first autumn in Milton, Tom went on a moose hunt with a borrowed rifle and with two experienced woodsmen as guides. He didn't shoot a moose, but he discovered "the marvellous freedom of the forest." He went hunting many times after that, and he learned the art of moose calling with a birchbark horn well enough to experience the thrill of enticing a great bull near him. But the success of the hunt was secondary. To Tom, the wilderness became a sanctuary where he could find peace and healing when his spirit was troubled and his nerves were frayed.

When that year's end came he had no thought of leaving Milton and the mill, even though his salary was a pittance and his work as an accountant was dull. Besides his new-found love of the wilderness, he had fitted easily into the simple country life. At his boarding house there was a piano, and to his own surprise the bugbear of his childhood became a real pleasure. He enjoyed playing old songs, just for fun, sometimes singing to his own accompaniment. Soon neighbours and friends came to listen. Tom's ears burned with pleasure when he overheard one of the villagers say,

"Nice fella. Plays pianna. Sings, too."

He was happy to be accepted on this basis. And in fact it was his enjoyment of music that lead to his courtship and marriage to Edith Freeman, the local music teacher, ". . . a petite and amusing chatterbox who played a good game of tennis and loved parties." Soon Tom and Edith were spending long evenings together, playing duets on the piano, laughing and singing with mutual delight. By the spring of 1926 they were engaged to be married.

Tom found an old Cape Cod farmhouse for sale almost next door to his fiancée's home. Luckily he still had most of his Sable Island savings and was able to meet the required $500.00 down payment. The house was in a state of neglect, so for the next year Tom camped in the kitchen while he repaired and re-decorated the whole establishment. It was ready to be occupied when he and Edith were married in June of 1927.

When the blissful honeymoon was over — spent in a cabin in the wilderness — they returned to Milton and bad news. The MacLeod Company had fallen on such hard times the mills had been closed and only a skeleton staff remained. Tom's salary had been cut again to

$100.00 a month. He feared he would soon be out of a job.

Word came from the Company's owner that baled pulp left on hand was to be sold at a sacrifice price. The manager, Austin Parker, was told to cut every cent of cost to get it loaded on a ship at nearby Liverpool. For this back-breaking work he and Tom laboured with the men. Austin Parker had become his best friend and Tom was willing to do anything to help him. Both men were young and in good physical condition from much time spent together tramping through the woods, but the work was prodigious. Tom observed:

> . . . Each bale had weighed 228 pounds when it came off the mill press but since then in the open sheds it had absorbed moisture and weighed up to three hundred pounds. These moist bales had now frozen together in their tiers to the shed roofs. Every bale had to be pried loose with peavies, manhandled down to the floor, placed on a big wheelbarrow, trundled up a gangway into a railway boxcar, and again stacked to the roof of the car.

At the end of a day at this work Tom had barely enough strength to trudge the three kilometres back home. He felt sorry for the poor labourers who worked alongside him for two dollars a day. He knew they were suffering from malnutrition because their meals consisted mainly of bread and molasses. Some men simply couldn't do the work and dropped out, exhausted, before the end of the first day.

Tom's anger gave him strength. Always his sympathy was for the "ordinary man," and his contempt was for "comfortable owners" who made themselves rich by exploiting helpless employees.

But Tom was upset by more than the work at the paper company. Edith was pregnant. Tom now realized, with a sense of despair, that he and his bride had very little in common. In the first glow of his love he had enjoyed going to house parties and amateur theatricals which were a way of life for the gregarious Edith; but now he found them utterly boring. In any case, he told her, there was no money for any sort of entertainment. It took every cent he earned just to pay for the food, the mortgage, and the insurance. And soon there would be an addition to the family.

CHAPTER 7

To Be a Writer

Somehow Tom had to earn more money. For the first time he thought seriously about trying to write and sell a short story for pay. He got out his rickety old typewriter and began to spend his evenings putting together another fictional story about Sable Island. He wrote and re-wrote it painstakingly and at last sent it off to "Canada's National Magazine," *Maclean's*. Back came a cheque for sixty dollars. What a windfall! And what a thrill of satisfaction! He had sold a story first time out to Canada's top magazine. Now he could do what he had always wanted to do— write stories with a clear conscience. Nobody could say that he was wasting his time.

Immediately he set to work upon another—a humorous story founded on fact. It was about an old Indian, nicknamed "Scabby Lou," who was stealing slabwood from the mill owner. Lou was repeatedly caught and warned, but he persisted in taking what he wanted without permission. The mill owner thought he knew how he could cure this bad habit. He bored tiny holes in some of the slabs and plugged them with bits of dynamite. One night Scabby Lou's stove blew up. The story was told, with shouts of laughter at poor Lou's expense, all over town. It was a great yarn, and Tom thought up a funny, satisfying ending. He sent it to *Maclean's*, confident that he would receive another nice cheque.

To his dismay the story was promptly returned with a scathing letter from the editor, saying that *Tit for Tat* was a silly, unbelievable tale. Tom was stunned. He knew the editor was wrong. He tore up the letter and threw the manuscript into his desk drawer. He vowed he would never — ever — send another story to that editor.

Tom had other problems to confront. Each night when he reached home he was greeted by Edith's unhappy face. He hoped that when the baby came things would be different. Edith had an affectionate nature and loved children. He was sure she would be happier when she had a child of her own.

But that spring the young Raddalls had to face heartbreak. In those days there was no hospital in Liverpool so babies were born at home, attended by the local doctor and midwife. After a long agonizing labour Edith's baby was born dead.

The next day, in a snowstorm, Tom went by himself to make arrangements for a funeral and was told that a stillborn child was buried without religious ceremony, because it had never lived. A man who ran a little shingle mill was also the coffin-maker. His hearse consisted of a black box on wheels, drawn by a draft horse. Tom went with him to the cemetery and watched while a tiny white coffin was placed in a hole and buried.

Edith had almost died with the baby. She said she never wanted to get pregnant again and face such a terrible ordeal, and Tom agreed that this would have to be so. His heart was heavy and he was so poor he couldn't even meet the payments on the house.

Just about this time, word came that the MacLeod Company was being squeezed out of existence by a huge paper mill, to be built, at a cost of fifteen million dollars, by a Nova Scotia born financier, Isaac Walton Killam. Construction immediately began on dam sites on the Mersey River for the manufacture of hydro-electric power, and also for a mill at Brooklyn, situated near the entrance to Liverpool Harbour.

Tom consulted with his friend, Austin Parker, and it was agreed that he should apply for a position with the new Mersey Paper Company. He was hired at once — but at the same miserable wage of $100.00 a month. However, he was promised a substantial raise as soon as he proved his worth.

When he began his new employment he had to walk eight kilometres to and from work every day, regardless of the weather. He had sold his bicycle and he couldn't afford even the cheapest second-hand car. In a way, he didn't mind walking. Ideas for stories were always simmering in his brain, and he got in the habit of composing plots and developing characters while on foot.

He had succeeded in establishing himself with a publisher of fast-paced "blood and thunder" stories for periodicals in the United States, and in this way was beginning to add to his meagre income. He was acutely aware that he was writing trash — "pot boilers" — as a way of earning extra money. But he also knew he was serving an apprenticeship and learning a great deal about the craft of story writing. A serial story, "Captain Moonlight," sold for $800.00. Tom used part of that cheque to buy Edith a fur coat. This was his way of seeking forgiveness for the many evenings he refused to attend the social amusements of the village, sitting instead at the kitchen table, scribbling away, oblivious to the world about him.

(Nova Scotia Government Department Services)
Foreground: Lobster traps and fishing boats.
Background: The Mersey Paper Mill, Brooklyn, Nova Scotia.

Tom's route to work led from Milton along the edge of the Mersey River, five kilometres southeast to the town of Liverpool, and then east along the coast another three kilometres to Brooklyn.

The real trouble was that the long walks were too time consuming. Tom needed to be nearer his workplace and he wanted all the time he could get to put his stories down on paper. The need to move to Liverpool was rapidly becoming apparent. Edith would enjoy the convenience of shops and the social life. For Tom, it was a town with an exciting history.

Liverpool was situated at the mouth of the Mersey River—which the Micmac called "Ogomkegeak," "The Going Out Place." The first settlers had all been New Englanders, pious, hardworking, hard drinking people "who thought the centre of the universe was Boston." Only fifteen years after its founding, the townspeople were almost literally caught in the crossfire of the American Revolution. Some wanted to join the rebels; others remained staunchly loyal to the British. All the controversy had been hushed up afterwards, and when the United States entered the War on the side of the French in 1812, Liverpool men were among the first to answer the call of the British Government to fit out their fishing schooners as privateers to prey on enemy shipping. They were wonderfully successful. One of these privateers, *The Liverpool Packet*, captured nearly a hundred American ships during the course of the War. It was a great way to make a lot of fast money. By the end of the eighteenth century, Liverpool had become one of the busiest and most prosperous ports in Nova Scotia.

Those great days were long since gone, but not entirely forgotten. Life moved at a leisurely pace. Silent reminders of the past were old cannon that marked the street corners. People talked about rusty muskets, powder horns and swords which were sometimes uncovered in attics and barns.

As a resident of Liverpool, Tom would have better access to colonial objects and documents. He would be able to borrow books from a small circulating library and from friends. Tom had already helped to form an historical society.

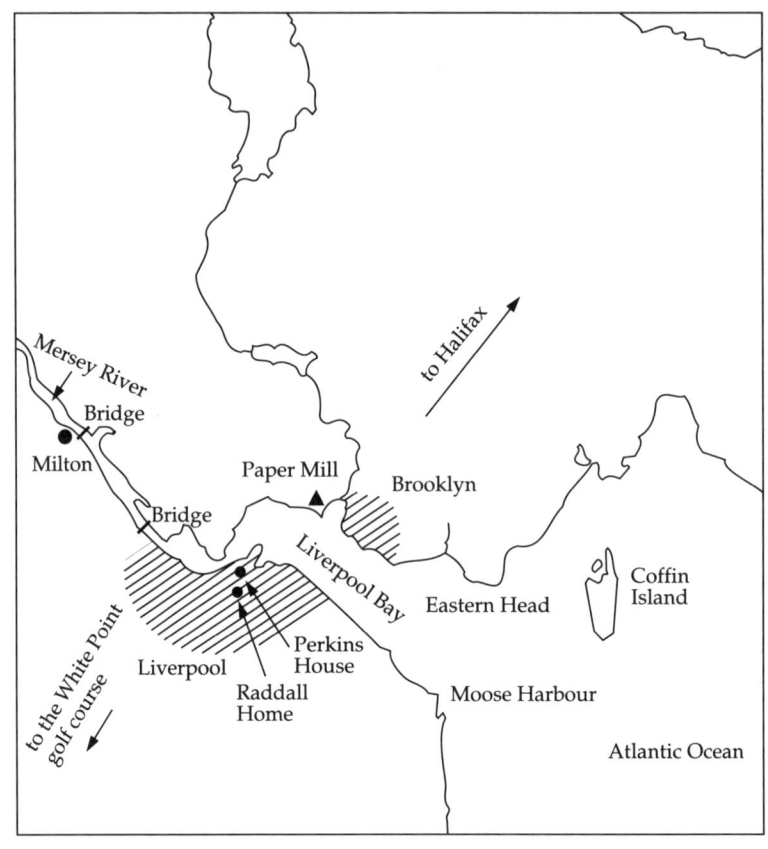

(This map is based on information taken from 21A/2 © 1976 Her Majesty the Queen in Right of Canada with permission of Energy, Mines, and Resources Canada.)

When Thomas Raddall first started to work at the Mersey Paper Mill, he walked from Milton almost to Brooklyn. After he made his permanent home in Liverpool, he often walked up the river to Milton, crossed the bridge and returned on the other side. During these long walks he plotted, planned, and created characters for his stories.

The true founder of the Historical Society was an old gentleman — Mr. Long — who had been born in Liverpool but had spent most of his life as a newspaperman in the United States. He loved to get back to his old home town and hunt around for stories and relics of history.

One evening he came to the Raddall home, bubbling with excitement.

"Tom, guess what I've found!"

"What?"

"Wait. Come on down to the town hall."

When they arrived, all Tom saw was a great bundle of old yellowed sheets of foolscap, covered with faded, spidery writing.

"What's this?"

"It's a diary, written by one of the early settlers of Liverpool — name of Simeon Perkins. I found the papers stashed away in a dusty old cupboard. Heaven knows how many years they've been there, quite forgotten. It's marvellous! It's a gold mine! The old guy has written about everything. He was one of the big shots of the town, with a finger in every pie, full of the liveliest interest and curiosity. Wait until you read it."

Tom couldn't wait, and soon there was silence in the dimly lit room except for the rustle of turning pages as the two men read on and on . . . carried back in time. . . .

"I guess they didn't take many baths in those days," said Tom, much later. "After all, it was so cold in the house in winter, sometimes Perkins couldn't even thaw out ink on the hearth so he could write. And listen to this:

"'November 16, 1777: I am curing the itch by an ointment of tarr, brimstone, and mutton tallow, put into a piece of canvas and hung in a corner to drain out, with which we oint our bodies at night. Sleep in my tarry clothes. Next night oint again and wash and put on clean cloathes.'"

Mr. Long laughed. Then his face grew sober.

"They had a smallpox outbreak here. People were so frightened and superstitious about vaccination they refused to have it done, and they were dying like flies. Horrible! But look here! Simeon Perkins was a wise, bold man. 'February 10, 1801. My family were inoculated by Mr. John Kirk, all in the left hand.'"

"The left hand!" exclaimed Tom. "What an awkward place to be vaccinated!"

His face grew even more serious, and he shuddered as he read another entry:

"'May 27, 1779: I was present at the flogging of a soldier, his name Dudgeon, 400 lashes. He was sentenced for being drunk and sleeping upon sentry. One Higgins was sentenced 250, I think for being drunk on duty.'"

Suddenly, in his mind's eye, Tom could envision again the tarred bodies of sailors gibbeted on the beach at McNab's Island. Perkins had made the entry casually, without comment. Evidently he felt that justice had been done. Yet Simeon Perkins was a pious, religious man . . . It was just that people thought differently in those days. . . .

Tom was reluctant to put the diary away, but he had to go to work at the mill in the morning.

Already Tom had formed a friendship with his new boss, Colonel Jones, a man he described as a "short brisk pot-bellied *bon vivant* and a very capable business man with ideas and interests as wide as the world."

The Colonel had bought a fishing schooner with a beaver carved in wood for a figurehead. He renamed the schooner *Awenishe,* the Ojibwa word for "Little Beaver." His idea was to use the yacht for entertaining customers, such as important paper executives, and he asked Tom to draw plans for a wireless outfit and act as operator when at sea. However, the Colonel's ideas didn't work out exactly as planned. The guests nearly all turned green with sea-sickness and begged to be put ashore at once; and the wireless outfit proved to be too expensive. All the same, for several summers Tom went on cruises aboard the "Little Beaver," making himself useful by taking the wheel or handling the sails whenever he was needed.

Tom loved sailing and the sea and he was learning all about the workings of a small sailing ship. This knowledge would prove invaluable for his writing.

In the course of their many conversations, the Colonel learned about Tom's interest in history and his work as an author. Always an opportunist, he decided to take advantage of his employee's talents.

When Tom told the Colonel about the discovery of the Simeon Perkins diary, the Colonel was intrigued.

"Few people know anything about Nova Scotia's early romantic history," Tom said.

The Colonel was fascinated.

"Why don't you write a book about it?" he asked.

"Because nobody would publish it," Tom retorted. "Not now, in 1930, when the whole world is in the depths of a depression. Publishers are going bankrupt every week."

But the Colonel's enthusiasm was not to be dimmed.

"I'll publish it," he said. "I know what! I'll use it to advertise our newsprint. And not just one book, Tom. You can write a whole series. Dozens of Nova Scotia sea stories! Start with the privateers of Liverpool . . . and then maybe go right back to the beginning of the coming of the Norsemen."

Tom's imagination caught fire, and in 1931 his first book was published. He called it *Saga of the Rover*—the heroic account of a famous Liverpool privateer. It was a great thrill to have a book of his own in print. Now he decided he'd follow the Colonel's advice and start at the beginning of Nova Scotia's history, with the arrival of the Norsemen.

The Colonel gave him time off to go to Halifax to do research in archives and libraries. Whenever he could visit Halifax, Tom always wandered down to his old haunts along the waterfront. As usual he walked with his mind full of ideas for his current story. This time, of course, he was dreaming about the Norsemen and what it must have been like to cross the cold and stormy North Atlantic in a tiny, square-rigged boat.

Suddenly he stopped in his tracks. He thought he must be dreaming. There, tied up at the wharf, was a Viking long-ship! It was just as he had pictured it in his imagination — a dragon's head at the bow, shields along the bulwarks — even the striped square sail.

It seemed too remarkable a coincidence to be true, but it really was a full-sized replica, built in Norway. Soon Tom was deep in conversation with the owner-skipper, who was surprised and delighted to meet a Canadian who was so knowledgeable about the ancient Viking voyagers. The ship was about to return to Norway. And the Captain offered Tom a berth!

Tom's heart leaped with joy. He had only to say "yes" and here was the high adventure he had always dreamed about. He almost accepted on the spot. Right then he wanted, more than anything, to turn his back upon his drab existence as a clerk at the paper mill, and go off to see the world.

But he hesitated. He asked to have one night to consider the matter. He would give his answer in the morning. All that night he lay awake, wrestling with his conscience, and when morning came he knew he had to say "no." He said afterwards it was the hardest decision he ever made in his life.

CHAPTER 8

Decision

On a frosty night in November 1934 Edith was safely delivered of a fine healthy baby boy. He was named Thomas Head Raddall III.

It was a happy occasion, but the baby had arrived too late to become an integral part of Tom's life. By this time he was leading not just a double life, but three distinctly separate lives.

There were the long hours at the office, when, dressed in a business suit, he worked methodically with the accounts of the Mersey Company. There were the long evenings, after he got home, when he worked far into the night writing his stories, living with his imaginary people, forgetful of the real world. And there were also long, wonderful weekends and holidays which he spent in the woods, forgetful of everything except the world of nature.

Not much time was left for his family.

During the summer of 1932, when Tom was sailing with the *Awenishe* and writing his second book, *The Markland Saga*, his two best friends, Austin Parker and Brenton Smith, were busy building a big log cabin at Eagle Lake ". . . for hunting, fishing, and just plain getting-away-from-it-all." That cabin was to be Tom's retreat, his safety-valve for many years to come.

(Courtesy Dalhousie University Archives, Thomas Raddall Papers)
J.A. Parker (left) and Thomas Raddall (right) at peace in the wilderness at Eagle Lake, Nova Scotia, in October, 1931.

The three had chosen a good place for a hideaway. That part of the forest was known as "Injun Devil Country," and was avoided by everyone, except one or two Indian trappers. Tom described it:

> At the south end of Eagle Lake was a swampy wild meadow called "the haunted bog," a natural place for moose calling like all such openings in the forest. Many years before us, a party of young hunters had bivouacked on a small wooded island in this swamp, intending to call moose in the morning. During the night, and again in the dim light of a misty dawn, they heard weird and frightful screams from something invisible rushing through the air about them. They cleared out in a hurry when full daylight came . . . They knew nothing whatever of *Windigo*, the evil spirit of the Ojibwas, which rushed through the air, making dreadful cries, but was never seen, or *Ska-de-ga-mut-k'* of Micmac legend, which does the same thing and is always a presage of death or disaster.

Fortunately Tom was not superstitious, and indeed he said that he and his friends never heard or saw anything frightful. He had even called for bull moose, by moonlight, on the haunted bog and heard nothing worse than his own voice bellowing through a birch-bark horn.

Because Tom came to know the Nova Scotia wilderness so intimately, he was able to write about it with fluid ease. It didn't matter whether he was describing it for a modern romance like *The Wings of Night,* or for historical novels like *His Majesty's Yankees.* The heart of the wilderness and its wildlife remained the same. When David Strang (*His Majesty's Yankees*) went moose hunting for the first time with Indian guides, Tom knew that the boy, who had lived so many generations before, must have experienced exactly the same emotions that he himself had felt on a similar occasion.

> There is no silence like the death quiet of our Nova Scotia woods on a frosty fall morning. Southward where the brook trickled over a ledge in a neck of the woods we could hear its water, a good mile. Somewhere in the mist a chickadee wakened, then another, and another, and their small bird voices pierced the silence like sharp little knives. A pair of meat jays came to us, flitting like small gray ghosts from branch to branch, inspecting us with bright, inquisitive eyes. . . .
>
> Again silence, but not for long. There was a tremendous splash from the mist over the brook. My heart thumped the breath out of me. It amazed me to realize how quietly the moose, that great, ungainly creature, can move when he so chooses. The big bull had crossed two hundred yards of wild meadow without a squelch, without a whisper of grass stalks, until the brook crossed his path, too deep to wade and too wide to jump. . . Now the mist seemed to roll like a wave of the sea, and out of the wave loomed a mighty figure, black and shapeless. . . .

But even with the short interludes spent in his beloved wilderness, Tom was finding his workload unbearable. Above all, he wanted time to write.

The Markland Saga had been published — 300 copies — but that was the last of the series. The Colonel had not paid one cent for all Tom's work as an author, and by this time Tom was enjoying some real literary success elsewhere.

A friend had given him a bundle of back numbers of a prestigious British publication, *Blackwood's Magazine*. Stories in these copies were of a literary quality and were written by authors living in almost every part of the English-speaking world except Canada. Tom was puzzled. Why weren't there any Canadian stories?

Overburdened with work at the office and deeply involved in the *Markland Saga*, he couldn't take time out to write another short story. Then he remembered *Tit for Tat*. He found the story of "Scabby Lou" in the back of a drawer where he had tossed it, several years before, after its rejection from *Maclean's*. He read it again. It was a good story. He put it into an envelope and mailed it overseas. Back came a letter of acceptance and a cheque for $90.00. And they wanted more!

After that Tom no longer wrote trash for the "pulps." Again he remembered his father's words, ". . . strive to make a name for yourself."

He became his own severest critic. He wrote and rewrote every sentence of every story. Soon he had reason to believe he could indeed make a name for himself — if only he had *time*! Already he had received praise in high places.

Noticing his stories in *Blackwood's Magazine*, Rudyard Kipling and John Buchan praised them warmly. The latter's friendship continued after he became Lord Tweedsmuir and Governor-General of Canada. In 1939 he said of Mr. Raddall's writing: "I confess to a special liking for a story which has something of a plot and which issues in a dramatic climax, a type which has had many distinguished exponents from Sir Walter Scott through [Robert Louis] Stevenson and [Guy de] Maupassant to [Rudyard] Kipling and [Joseph] Conrad. To this school Mr. Raddall belongs, and he is worthy of a great succession. He has the rare gift of swift, spare, clean-limbed narrative. And he has great stories to tell."

Encouraged and inspired by such praise, Tom began to hate and resent his dull routine work at the Mersey Paper Company. Often he was so tired he had no time or energy left for his writing. One night he wrote in his diary:

> . . . After a bad night the day in the office is a long agony and I find myself making stupid mistakes . . . Sometimes I think I must give up writing, or give up working for the paper company, or go mad.

He had to take a chance — a bold, unprecedented choice. One day he walked into the Mersey Paper Company and tendered his resignation. He had determined to make his living solely by his pen.

Up to that time no Canadian author of fiction had been able to earn even a subsistence income. Two of the best known Canadian writers, Charles G.D. Roberts and Marshall Saunders, had become indigent in their old age, dependent on the charity of others. Thomas Raddall would never let that happen to him or to his family. He had enough saved so that he was quite sure that they could manage somehow for three years. That was the time he allowed to prove himself.

And Edith — that good and loyal woman — agreed. There were two babies in the family now. Tommy had a little sister, Frances, born in 1936, and the children had become the most important part of their mother's world. She would make many sacrifices for them in the years to come.

Tom was not a demonstrative person but he appreciated his wife's efforts. Later he wrote to a friend:

> My wife was wonderful. "Pinching and scraping" is not only a trite phrase but a term utterly inadequate for what she accomplished, not only then but in the first few years after 1938, when I threw up my job and launched forth as a professional writer.

The Colonel tried to keep Tom in his employ. He suggested that Tom should just take a year's leave of absence from his job, certain at the end of that time he would be very grateful to return.

But Tom refused.

> "I discovered, long ago on Sable Island, that I couldn't learn to swim with one hand clinging to the side of a boat."

He wrote in his diary:

> Ambition is an uncomfortable disease. Perhaps I shall regret my lightly resigned job before three years are out, but I know I shall never regret this attempt to establish myself as a writer.

Tom had to have complete solitude, away from the distractions of children's chatter, telephone conversations, and the visits of neighbours, so a sound-proof study was built at the rear of his house. But he couldn't bear to be boxed in. Five windows gave him views he enjoyed ". . . a pond where frogs sang in spring, and a tall wood of spruce trees where many birds nested in summer."

(A.F.W. Consultants)
Thomas Raddall and the painting of Scabby Lou, 1985.

On one wall of his study he hung a large painting of an old Indian with a pair of oxen. The man represented Scabby Lou. Tom had become owner of the picture in a curious way, and it was the best reminder in the world to help him keep faith in his ability as a writer, no matter what editors or critics might say.

The painting was a gift from his old 'adversary,' Napier Moore, the editor of *Maclean's* magazine. Without asking permission, an author's agent in London had taken the liberty of sending tear-sheets of two of Thomas Raddall's short stories published in *Blackwood's* to *Maclean's*. One of the stories was *Tit for Tat*. The

Maclean's editor bought both stories. He had forgotten all about his contemptuous rejection of the "Scabby Lou" story. The agent sent Tom a cheque, first taking a 10% commission for himself.

Tom was outraged. He didn't want any story of his published in *Maclean's* at any price, and he wrote the editor to this effect. Mr. Moore was shocked and very upset. He pleaded with Tom to change his mind. He said he had bought the stories in good faith from the London agent, and he had already commissioned a well-known artist to illustrate *Tit for Tat*.

In the end Tom relented and the story was printed. As a gesture of gratitude and good will from *Maclean's*, he was given the painting. After all, Thomas Raddall had now been recognized by top critics as a master of the craft of the short story.

CHAPTER 9

The Price of Success

Now that he could write full time, Tom was selling steadily to *Blackwood's* and also to the *Saturday Evening Post,* then the top-paying American periodical. His friend, Lord Tweedsmuir, urged him to have a collection of his short stories published. In 1939, the year that the Second World War broke out, *The Pied Piper of Dipper Creek* appeared in print. Five years later *The Pied Piper* was given the highest recognition in Canada — the Governor-General's Award.

At the beginning of the War, Tom tried to enlist for active service but was told — to his chagrin — that he was too old.

Back at his desk he worked all the harder. He put short stories aside, a field in which he had already proved his worth. (In 1941 he earned $4500.00 from writing short stories — more than twice what he would have earned working at the job he hated with the Mersey Paper Company.) He decided to try another form of writing — a book-length novel. He found it a very different kind of work. His first effort — a novel about lumbering and the paper mill — ended in the waste basket, after months of hard labour.

But another daring idea had been nagging at his conscience for a long time. As he had read and studied the Perkins Diary, an unexpected truth had been revealed to him. It had to do with Nova Scotia at the time of the American Revolution. Tom had been taught in school, and in everything he had read on the subject since, that, during the War, Nova Scotians had all remained staunchly loyal to the British crown.

Now he knew this was not true. The history books had lied. He knew, because honest Simeon Perkins had recorded all that had happened in those unhappy times — and Perkins had been there. Tom decided to tell the facts in the form of a novel which he was sure would come as a surprise to the academic world.

When *His Majesty's Yankees* was published in both Canada and the United States, it received acclaim everywhere. *The New York Times Book Review* called it "the historical novel discovery of the year."

The townspeople of Liverpool were astonished and delighted. They all united to honour the Liverpool man who had made their town famous and gave him a fine barometer with the inscription:

Presented to Thomas H. Raddall
by his fellow townsmen
in affection and esteem.

Tom's heart was warmed. Perhaps that token from his own friends meant more to him than any of the many national and international honours he was to receive in the future. Nova Scotia was his home. These were his people. He had a great and abiding love for his own province. In fact, he never wrote about any other place in all the years that he earned his living by writing.

When he went to Toronto to accept one of the three Governor-General's Awards he was to be given, he was

(Courtesy Dalhousie University Archives, Thomas Raddall Papers)
Tom and Edith on the White Point golf course near Liverpool, Nova Scotia.

offended by members of the writing community who almost always greeted the fact that he came from Nova Scotia with some slightly sneering or jocular remark, such as,

"How are the codfish down there?"

In spite of the honour he received, he didn't enjoy that visit to "Upper Canada." He couldn't wait to get home again to his own people, his own land, and his own desk. And — for the most part — that's where he stayed.

Many of his fellow townspeople thought that Tom Raddall had chosen an easy way of life. He was his own boss; he could do as he pleased; and anyway he liked to scribble stories. When did he work? Any afternoon he could be seen going for long walks or sometimes golfing in summer, or maybe just idling down by the pier, gossiping with the fishermen. Later, when he had built a little cabin of his own at Moose Harbour, he often stayed there alone — doing nothing, some said. What about his family?

In fact Thomas Raddall worked incredibly long hours and he had to practise enormous self-discipline. It was true that, like many dedicated artists, he did not spend a lot of time with his family. He said himself that he was a loner, and perhaps should never have married.

Edith was almost a single parent. It was not until Tom and Frances were grown up and had children of their own, that they realized they hardly knew the father who had always shared their home.

Yet at times he had given them memorable surprises. When Tommy was about ten, he wanted desperately to join the school band. He begged his mother for a trumpet, but she told him sadly that they had no money for such things. Tommy was bitterly disappointed but he never thought of discussing possibilities with his father. One afternoon soon after this, when he came home from school and went up to his bedroom, a shining new trumpet lay on his bed—a gift from his father. Years later young Tom reflected,

"I was so happy I cried."

One winter a great blizzard came and the children were snowbound. They became restless and bored.

"I wish it was summer," said little Frances. "Then Daddy could take us on a picnic."

Her father laughed.

"I'll tell you what we'll do," he said. "We'll pretend it's summer. Your mother has house plants scattered all over the house. Let's collect them and put them all in my study. Then it will look just like summer, with green things growing all around. Mummy will make sandwiches, and we'll have a winter picnic."

That was a fun time the children never forgot.

Always the shadowy spectre of possible failure along with the fear he might not be able to meet his deadlines lurked behind Tom's shoulder as he worked. He wanted to achieve literary success, but he had to have financial success, as well. He thought the greatest gift he could give to his children would be the formal education he himself had missed. He was determined to build up his income so that he could send them to University, and it was partly for this reason that he worked himself to exhaustion.

He was so depleted physically and emotionally in the spring of 1944 when he completed his second novel, *Roger Sudden*, that he almost committed suicide. He was recovering from a severe bout of the flu which left him so depressed that nothing seemed worthwhile. One night he took his father's old Webley revolver, loaded it, and put it on his desk. For a long time he sat staring at it, but finally put it away. Remembering his father's

(Courtesy Dalhousie University Archives, Thomas Raddall Papers)
Tom and Edith working on a manuscript in his study.

courageous and hopeful spirit, he was ashamed of his own despair.

In January 1946 Tom wrote in his diary:

> This is the pattern of my life these winter days. I wake at 5 A.M. or more rarely at 6, and lie abed till 7 thinking of my novel and other matters. Then I get up, shake the coal furnace, light the oil stove in my den, and make my breakfast. I am at my desk by the time Edith and the kids get up.
>
> I read over yesterday's work, look up various bits of information, write a sentence or two, ponder a great deal, write a little more, ponder again, walk up and down, look at the snow outside for half an hour at a stretch (seeing a small brig in the West Indies.) Towards 10 A.M. I emerge from my den, still in pyjamas and

dressing gown, tend the furnace, wash and dress. At 11 A.M. I return to my desk and find that my mind now had gathered itself for a spurt. From then until noon I write perhaps 500 words, seldom more.

At noon the kids come home from school and Edith knocks sharply on my study door. I join them at dinner. Afterwards I listen to the news . . . and go upstairs and shave. If the day and the road are fit I put on my walking shoes, my old fur-collared blue pea-jacket, my old brown hat (a cap on windy days), gloves or mittens, and sally forth . . .

After supper I tend the furnace, dump ashes etc. About 7.30 I am back at my desk. The process of the morning is repeated.

As time went on, Tom's left hand, which had been deeply cut at the time of the Explosion and injured again later, began to give out. Eventually it became almost useless, and before he finished typing his remarkable history, *Halifax, Warden of the North*, he could type only with his right hand. Edith came to the rescue by learning the skill herself, and from then on she always typed the final versions of his manuscripts.

CHAPTER 10

A Name for Himself

With his award-winning history of Halifax completed Tom began to concentrate his energies on a novel that had long been in his mind—a very different book than any he had written before—*The Nymph and the Lamp*.

Although he calls the strange, lonely island "Marina," the locale really is Sable Island. Based on some of his unforgettable personal experiences, a powerful, haunting romance unfolds. Thomas Raddall considers *The Nymph and the Lamp* the best of his novels.

Whenever he finished a book Tom felt drained and exhausted, but he could never rest for long. When a new idea refused to present itself immediately, his conscience nagged. Despite all the recognition he had received and the comfort of achieving financial success, he felt guilty unless he was writing.

In the spring of 1951, when he was suffering from such a writer's block, he had a log cabin built for himself at Moose Harbour, on the west side of Liverpool Bay. It was near enough to his home that he could work during the day, but away from the telephone and from autograph hunters who had begun to plague him. He loved the little cabin and its peaceful surroundings, but that summer the words came slowly and painfully.

December of 1952 crept up before he was satisfied with *Tidefall* — which at one stage he said despairingly might have to be titled "Tomfall."

It was not until 1958 that Tom could afford to travel overseas, with Edith, for a much-needed holiday. He left her briefly in England and went on a lone pilgrimage, to Amiens, to the grave of his father.

> Now I stood there myself, almost forty years after the battle. The maple saplings planted soon after 1918 had grown to fine trees. There was a soft green turf underfoot, and on each grave a few sprigs of a modest little creeping plant with pink flowers called London Pride, nothing else. When I came to Dad's grave I fell on my knees and closed my eyes, not praying but simply thinking deeply of the stern soldier, warm at heart, whom I had seen last when I was twelve years old. . .
>
> It was time to leave, and I knew I was leaving for ever. At the entrance to the little cemetery I turned about and faced the graves, drawing myself up instinctively and saluting them all, with my eyes full of tears, thinking how young and brave these men had been, and how lonely they are now, forgotten, thousands of miles from home, in a world that considers 1918 as remote as the Crusades.
>
> It was the first time I had wept since I was a child.

Back in Canada Tom was soon hard at work again. In the following ten years he published three novels — *The Rover, The Governor's Lady, Hangman's Beach* — and a collection of short stories entitled *Footsteps on Old Floors*. Then, in 1970, during a radio interview, he dismayed his devoted listeners by making an unexpected announcement. *Footsteps on Old Floors* would be his final book.

Tom gave his reason. He said that many good and great writers had continued to create in old age after they had "suffered a waning of their powers." He had resolved, long before, that he was going to quit while his work was still in good repute.

Thomas Head Raddall had reached and surpassed all the goals he had set for himself. He no longer had financial worries. His son, Tom, had graduated from University and was now comfortably established as a dentist in his home town of Liverpool. Frances was happily married to a doctor and lived in New Brunswick.

Thomas Raddall was tired. All his life he had practised unrelenting self-discipline. He had worked incredibly long hours. For years his habit, at the beginning of each November, had been to seal himself off in his sound-proof studio. From then on he lived only in his imaginary world with the characters of his own creation. Often he didn't know what day of the week it was. He had no idea what was going on in the outside world or even in his own household. When he emerged for long walks in the afternoons, he was still oblivious to the world about him.

Of course he had not always stayed in his studio. Altogether he had spent years of his life in research. Tom was meticulous about every detail in his work. Before he wrote *His Majesty's Yankees* (retold for young people in *Son of the Hawk*), he went to Beauséjour, so he could feel the cold and know what it was like to tramp about the damp marshes. He visited archives to study architecture, and learn the importance of the kitchen to the family in early Nova Scotia. By reading many old letters, he mastered the dialect of his people and came to understand how they thought, and how they socialized. He borrowed books on costumes from libraries so he knew exactly how his characters should be dressed. He drew maps and plans and diagrams of guns and battlefields. So carefully did he research, his historical accuracy has never been questioned.

Whenever Tom had completed one of his books, he was emotionally and physically drained. More than once he had been on the edge of a nervous breakdown, so he took time off to relax and do the things he liked best. He spent long weeks in the woods alone or with close friends, and then came home to take his wife and children on picnics to nearby white sand beaches, or to a favourite spot in the bush where he could dig for arrowheads and other Indian artifacts. And he and Edith spent hours together on the golf course.

Now that he was nearing seventy he changed the pattern of his life. He wanted time to look back, to live in retrospect, to write his memoirs without the pressure of a deadline. Besides the frustrations and sometimes agonizing periods when he had struggled with his work, he had other wonderfully satisfying things to remember.

How strange it had been when he had received his first honorary doctorate from Dalhousie University! For awhile whenever anyone addressed him as "Doctor" he had had an absurd impulse to look around for someone with a little black bag. Now he was accustomed to the title. The boy who had been forced to leave school in Grade Ten held degrees from four Universities.

Some honours he had refused. In 1968 he was asked to accept the position of Lieutenant-Governor of Nova Scotia, but he declined. Privately he and his wife had laughed about the invitation. There was nothing that Tom would have loathed more than having to dress up in formal attire and preside at ceremonial affairs.

Yet he had gladly accepted nearly all the highest honours his country could bestow upon an author.

(Courtesy Dalhousie University Archives, Thomas Raddall Papers)
Thomas Raddall receiving the insignia of an Officer of the Order of Canada from Governor General Michener at Ottawa in October, 1971.

Three times he had been chosen for the annual Governor-General's Award for Literature. He had been elected a Fellow of the Royal Society of Canada and had received both the Lorne Pierce Medal and the Gold Medal of the University of Alberta for Distinguished Service to Canadian Literature. He was entitled to wear the insignia of an Officer of the Order of Canada. His books had been published and read in countries all over the world.

Thomas Head Raddall had made a name for himself.

Appendix

Honours and Awards

1944 Governor-General's Literary Award
    for *The Pied Piper of Dipper Creek*
1949 Honorary Doctor of Laws
    Dalhousie University
    Governor-General's Literary Award for Creative Non-Fiction
    Halifax, Warden of the North
    (CBC Radio) first prize in Radio Awards
    "Canada's Heritage of Sail"
1951 Boy's Club of America Junior Book Award
    Son of the Hawk
1953 Elected Fellow of the Royal Society of Canada
1956 Lorne Pierce Medal for "Distinguished Service to Canadian Literature"
1958 Governor-General's Award for History
    The Path of Destiny
1960 Doubleday Canada Novel Prize
    The Governor's Lady
1969 Honorary D. Litt. from
    St Mary's University
1971 Officer of the Order of Canada

1972 Honorary D.C.L.
       University of King's College
1973 Honorary LL.D.
       St. Francis Xavier University
1977 Gold Medal of the University of Alberta for "Distinguished Service to Canadian Literature"
1984 The T.H. Raddall prize, established by the Bowater Mersey Paper Company Limited to promote historical research and literary excellence among high school students across western Nova Scotia
1989 The gold medal of the City of Halifax entitled *Award of Merit: Literary Excellence*
1989 Acadia University announced establishment of the *Thomas Raddall Symposium in Atlantic Literature*, to begin in 1990
1989 The city of Halifax named and opened the Thomas Raddall Library
1989 Hollywood film producer began preliminary work on a major motion picture from Raddall's novel, *The Nymph and the Lamp*

NOVELS

(in chronological order of first publication)
Saga of the Rover   1931
His Majesty's Yankees   1942
Roger Sudden   1944
Pride's Fancy   1946
The Nymph and the Lamp   1950
Son of the Hawk   1950
Tidefall   1953
The Wings of Night   1956
The Rover: The Story of a Canadian Privateer   1958
The Governor's Lady   1960
Hangman's Beach   1966

Short Story Collections

The Pied Piper of Dipper Creek and Other Tales   1939
Tambour and Other Stories   1945
The Wedding Gift and Other Stories   1947
A Muster of Arms and Other Stories   1954
At the Tide's Turn and Other Stories   1959
The Dreamers   1986

Juvenile

Courage in the Storm   1987

Histories

The Markland Sagas   1934
West Novas: A History of the West Nova Scotia Regiment   1948
Halifax, Warden of the North   1948
The Path of Destiny: Canada from the British Conquest to Home Rule 1763-1850   1957
Footsteps on Old Floors: True Tales of Mystery   1968
This Is Nova Scotia, Canada's Ocean Playground   1970
The Mersey Story   1979

Memoir

In My Time   1976

ABOUT THE AUTHOR

Joyce Barkhouse shares with Thomas Raddall a love of the romantic history of her native Nova Scotia. Inspired by Raddall's first novels, *His Majesty's Yankees* and *Roger Sudden*, she began to write short historical fiction of her own, mostly for children. Now a widow, she lives alone in Halifax in winter, and in a cottage on a cliff overlooking the turbulent Bay of Fundy in summer. She is the author of seven books, and is working on another, a partly fictional story of her early childhood.

OTHER BOOKS BY JOYCE BARKHOUSE

George Dawson, the little giant
Pit Pony
The Witch of Port LaJoye
The Lorenzen Collection
Abraham Gesner
Anna's Pet (with Margaret Atwood)